CASTLES

FACTS • THINGS TO MAKE • ACTIVITIES

RACHEL WRIGHT

SEA-TO-SEA

Mankato Collingwood London

This edition first published in 2005 by
Sea-to-Sea Publications
1980 Lookout Drive
North Mankato
Minnesota 56003

Copyright © Sea-to-Sea Publications 2005

ISBN   1-932889-04-3

Printed in China

Library of Congress Control Number: 2004103596

2 4 6 8 9 7 5 3

Published by arrangement with the Watts Publishing Group Ltd, London

Editor: Hazel Poole
Consultants: Dr. Michael Thompson, Brian Davison
Designed by: Sally Boothroyd
Artwork by: Jeremy Semmens
Photography by: Chris Fairclough
Additional picture research by: Juliet Duff

CONTENTS

SAFE HOUSES

During the Middle Ages — which lasted from about the 700s to 1500 AD — there were thousands of castles in western Europe. They were owned by kings, lords and barons. Castles were a symbol of power, authority and defense. Although many of these castles were never even threatened with attack, all were designed to repel the weapons of their day. They were like homely forts, built to protect their owner and his land, his family, his servants, his craftspeople and his private army of knights.

CASTLE SITES

Where possible, castles were built on or near natural defenses such as cliffs and coastlines. Many were founded near the port, town or crossroads they were designed to protect or control. Some were built near rivers and streams. A ditch could then be dug around the finished castle and the water diverted into it. These water-filled ditches, called moats, made castles much harder to attack.

▲ *This painting of Lusignan Castle in France is taken from the Duke of Berry's* The Book of Hours *which was made in 1400.*

▶ *Many wooden castles had gatehouses and movable bridges to guard the main entrance and the approach to the tower.*

Castles were often closely linked with a neighboring town or village. As well as being a rich man's home, they acted as a tax office, administration center, courthouse and prison for local villagers.

WOODEN CASTLES

In some parts of Europe, the first castles were made of earth and wood. Often a steep-sided flat topped mound of earth was dug, surrounded by a ditch. A wooden tower was then built on top of the mound and encircled by a timber fence. This tower was the strong point of the castle and the place where valuables were kept.

The castle's owner and his family slept in apartments beside the Great Hall, in the courtyard below. The rest of the domestic buildings, including the kitchen, the chapel and the stables, also stood in the courtyard. These buildings were usually timber-framed and plastered over with earth and animal dung. The more important ones were roofed with tiles or shingles. The others were thatched with reeds or straw.

◀ The castle at Peñafiel in Spain was built on top of a rocky ridge for protection. "Peña fiel" means "faithful rock."

Wooden castles were cheaper, quicker and required less skill to build than stone ones, but they had two major disadvantages. They rotted and burned easily. For those who wanted a more permanent home, the only solution was to build in stone.

5

PULP AND PAPER CASTLES

You will need: newspaper • wallpaper paste • glue brush • large bowl of warm water • corrugated cardboard • scissors • ruler • pencil • glue • paint • some wood or chipboard to use as a baseboard • toothpicks.

1. Soak a sheet of newspaper in warm water. Squeeze the water out, and lay the paper flat on your baseboard.

▲**2.** Cover one side of the paper with wallpaper paste. Scrunch it up and knead it into a pulp. Repeat this process until you have enough pulp to model your castle's mound and courtyard. If you want to save time, mold your mound over an old plastic tub or cup.

3. When your model is finished, leave it somewhere warm to dry.

TO MAKE A TOWER FOR THE MOUND

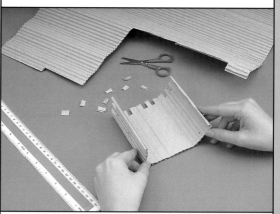

▲**4.** Fold a rectangle of corrugated cardboard, as shown. Check that the outside ridges are vertical and that the four main panels are the same width.
Cut evenly spaced notches along the top of the tower, too.

TO MAKE THE ROOF

▲**5.** Draw a square with sides the same length as the width of one of the tower's panels. Add four tabs and cut this shape out.

▲**6.** Fold the tabs down and smear them with glue. Now fold the tower around its roof. Make sure that the roof lies below the notches. Glue the rest of the tower together and paint it.

▲**8.** Following your markings, cut away the top of the cardboard. Cover the tab with glue and bend the building into shape.

TO MAKE THE ROOF

9. Cut out a small piece of cardboard. Fold it in half and glue it into place.

10. When you have made as many buildings as you need, paint them. Stick dried grass, straw or twine onto their roofs.

11. When it has dried, paint your model and arrange the castle's buildings on it. Cut strips of corrugated cardboard for fences and glue them into position.

TO MAKE THE COURTYARD BUILDINGS

▲**7.** Measure and mark a rectangle of corrugated cardboard, as shown. The narrower panels must be the same width, as must the wider panels.

STONE STRONGHOLDS

No two castles were ever built alike. Castle design varied according to where the castle was built, what it was built with, and who was in charge of its construction. Even so, like their wooden counterparts, many early stone castles were designed around one tall tower. These stone towers, later known as keeps, were the last retreat of the castle. They could be defended even if the thick curtain walls surrounding the castle had been breached.

The keep at Hedingham Castle in Essex, England is still standing, even though it was built in 1140. The cutaway picture below shows what it may have looked like when its lordly owner was home and entertaining important guests.

To find out more about what went on in each room, turn the page.

Due to the risk of fire, many castle kitchens were built in the courtyard instead of the keep.

WELCOME TO HEDINGHAM

The main door was on the first floor to keep it beyond the reach of enemies with battering rams. Just to be on the safe side, it was also protected by a small tower and a wood and metal grating, called a portcullis. When unwanted visitors arrived, the portcullis was slid down from above, to block the doorway.

Troublemakers ended up in the dungeon! They were probably lowered to their doom through a trapdoor in the ceiling.

ON THE GROUND FLOOR

The ground floor was the ideal place for storing food and drink because it was cool and dark. With no heating, and walls 12ft thick, the temperature was always low.

Unlike some keeps, Hedingham's had only one well. As there was no plumbing system, the water had to be carried to wherever it was needed. When someone wanted a bath, water had to be hauled upstairs, heated over a fire and poured into a large wooden tub.

THE SPIRAL STAIRCASE

A keep's floors were connected by a spiral staircase. Hedingham's stairs wind upward to the right. This may have helped a descending soldier if he had to fight his way down the stairs.

THE CONSTABLE'S ROOM AND THE LORD'S APARTMENT

The constable, who was in charge of the running of the castle, lived with his servants on the first floor. Here he greeted visitors and sorted out day-to-day castle business.

The most magnificent room of all was the lord's apartment, on the second floor. This was the room he used to carry out his public duties and to entertain formally. Rich tapestries hung on the walls to give the room color and help keep out drafts.

Far less magnificent, however, were the drafty toilets called garderobes. These were tiny rooms with chutes that ran through the walls and out into a pit at the bottom. The keep's floors were covered with rushes and sweet-smelling herbs to try and hide the terrible smell coming from the garderobes.

UP ON TOP

The lord, his family and their personal servants slept in the most private room of all, on the top floor. However, if the king came to stay, he would have been given this room, and the lord would have been relegated to the floor below.

The higher floors had large windows because they were out of enemy and burglar reach. The lower floors had to have narrower windows, and arrow slits so that defending archers could fire out without enemy archers firing in.

MAKE YOUR OWN TAPESTRY

Tapestry in the Middle Ages was usually woven on a loom like this.

You will need: a piece of thick cardboard ● scissors ● pencil ● ruler ● different colored spools of thread, yarn, string, raffia, strips of fabric, etc.

1. To make a simple loom, cut evenly spaced notches along the top and bottom edges of a piece of the cardboard.

▲**2.** Wind some yarn onto the cardboard and knot the ends to the outside notches. These are the warp threads. They need to be pulled fairly taut so that the cardboard bends slightly.

▲**3.** To keep the edges of your tapestry straight, draw lines inside the first and last warp threads. These lines will help you to see whether you are pulling your weaving too tight.

A thread that weaves in and out of the warp is called the weft.

▲ **4.** Tie your first weft to one of the outer warp threads. Weave it across the loom by going over and under alternate warp threads.

▲ **5.** When you reach the final warp thread, weave the weft back again. This time it needs to go under and over alternately.

6. As you weave backwards and forwards, push the weft threads down firmly with your fingers. This is so the warp won't show through.

7. When you want to change the color or thread, knot the old and new weft threads together and push the knot to the back of your tapestry.

8. When you have finished, lift your weaving off its cardboard loom. Slide a stick through the loops at the top and hang it up.

In Search of the Perfect Castle

Castle design did not stop with the keep. As the Middle Ages progressed, many designers tried to keep attackers out of the castle courtyard by building stronger curtain walls. These walls had towers jutting out from them at fairly close intervals. This made it possible for archers to shelter in the towers and fire along the face of the wall.

Some of the larger wall towers were also turned into mini keeps. They provided extra room and could be defended if the rest of the castle was captured.

A castle's weakest spot — its entrance — was also strengthened. During the early 1200s, much mightier twin-towered gatehouses were built over the entrance. These gatehouses often had comfortable rooms upstairs where the constable in charge of the castle household might live.

The less welcoming entrance passage below was guarded by a drawbridge over the moat, wooden gates and at least one portcullis. "Murder holes" in the roof of the passage enabled defenders to drop missiles on the enemy, and to pour water on any fires they might have lit against the gates.

Sometimes the approach to a gatehouse was protected by a long narrow passage called a barbican. This made it difficult for large numbers of attackers to reach the gates or to smash through them with a battering ram.

A castle with such strong, well-protected outer walls and towers clearly had no need for a keep. Instead, the great hall, chapel, stores and kitchens were built inside the castle's courtyard, along with the rest of the domestic buildings. This gave everyone far more room than they would have had in a keep.

During the late 1200s, European castle designers started to build concentric castles. These had an open space at their center and two sets of curtain walls. The inner wall overlooked the outer one. This enabled archers on the inner wall to fire at an approaching enemy over the heads of those defending the outer wall. If the enemy managed to cross the outer wall, he had no cover from the archers on the inner wall.

With every part defended by another part, concentric castles seemed almost impossible to capture.

▶ Beaumaris is Britain's finest concentric castle.

14

CREATE A CASTLE

You will need: cardboard • scissors • craft knife • ruler • pencil • tape • plastic straw • needle and thread • clay • poster board • paper clips • paint • pen • some small cardboard boxes, for example, empty tea bag boxes • gummed paper tape • glue • old toothbrush.

Ask a grown-up to help you with this, as the knife blade will be sharp!

Cardboard is easier to fold if it has been scored first. To do this, gently run the tip of your craft knife along the line you want to fold. Use a ruler when scoring straight lines.

TO MAKE THE GATEHOUSE

▲ **1.** Cut out a rectangle of cardboard. Divide it into four panels with a tab at one end, and then score all four lines.

2. To make battlements, cut evenly spaced notches along the top of the cardboard.

▲ **3.** Cut a door into the bottom edge of the first and third panels.

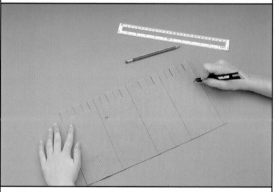

▲ **4.** Ask a grown-up to help you pierce a small hole in the left-hand side of the second panel, and another in the right-hand side of the fourth panel. The distance between each hole and its nearest panel must be the same. The distance between each hole and the base of the tower must also be the same. The holes must be just big enough for a straw to fit through them.

5. Cover the tab with glue, fold the tower into shape, and stick it together. Push a straw through both holes.

16

▲ **6.** Cut out a small piece of cardboard for the drawbridge. Use two tiny strips of tape to attach it to the doorway furthest from the straw.

▲ **7.** Thread a needle and knot the two loose ends of thread. Push the needle through one of the drawbridge's outer corners, and up through the front wall of the gatehouse.

▲ **8.** Lower the drawbridge and gently pull the thread straight. Now tape the rest of the thread to the straw. Make a second drawbridge rope in the same way.

9. Stick flattened strips of clay to the bottom of the drawbridge. It will now rise or lower when you turn both ends of the straw.

TO MAKE THE GATEHOUSE ROOF

▲ **10.** Measure the width of one of your gatehouse's panels. Draw a square with sides this same length onto some cardboard. Add four tabs and cut the shape out.

11. Score the lines you've drawn. Fold the tabs down, smear them with glue, and stick the roof into place.

TO MAKE WALL TOWERS

▲ **12.** Cut battlements along the top of a rectangle of poster board. Roll the light cardboard into a tube and hold it together with paper clips.

▲ **13.** Stand the tower on another piece of poster board and draw around it. Add tabs to your drawing and cut out this shape.

▲ **14.** Score the circle and cover its tabs with glue. Fold the tower around its roof and glue the two free edges together.

TO MAKE WALLS

▲ **15.** Cut battlements along the top of a long length of cardboard.

Cut another piece of cardboard, as long as the first but not quite as tall.

Cut two strips of cardboard. They must be the same length as your first piece, but only a quarter of its height.

▲ **16.** Mark tabs along the longer edges of both of the thinner strips of cardboard. All the tabs must be the same width.

▲ **17.** Score all the lines you've drawn. Fold the tabs down, cover them with glue and stick all four lengths ▼ of cardboard together, as shown.

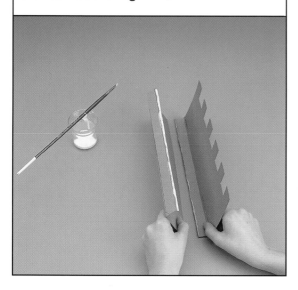

18. When you have made all the walls and towers you need, join them together with gummed paper. Tape two tall towers on either side of the gatehouse.

▲ **19.** Now paint your model. If you want the walls to look speckled, cover everything around the castle, including the floor, with newspaper. Dip an old toothbrush in watery paint, and run your thumb towards you along the bristles. The paint will spatter onto the walls.

TO MAKE THE DOMESTIC BUILDINGS

▲ **20.** Draw a line across the front of a small cardboard box. Then draw a diagonal line on each side of the box, as shown.
If the box has a lid, glue it shut.

▲21. Cut along these lines and lift up the flap. Now cut away the triangular areas on each side of the flap.

▲22. Straighten the flap and glue it onto the lower section of the box. You may find that you need to trim this roof.

23. To make a hall with two sloping roofs, simply glue two box buildings back to back.

24. When you have made as many buildings as you need, paint them.

TO MAKE A MOAT

▶ **25.** Stand your castle walls on a large sheet of blue cardboard. Draw a squiggly line around the edge of the cardboard. Draw a line around the inner walls of the castle's courtyard, too.

26. Remove the cardboard from under the castle and cut along both lines. To finish, slide your moat into place and arrange the domestic buildings in the courtyard.

CASTLES UNDER ATTACK

TRICKS AND SURPRISES

The best way to capture a castle was to take it by surprise. In 1204 a French soldier terrified the inhabitants of Château Gaillard by climbing up a garderobe chute and letting his comrades in through a window. Imagine the shock of going to the bathroom late one night, only to find someone climbing out of the seat!

GOING OVER THE TOP

Where a surprise attack failed, a direct assault might succeed. If the castle had a ditch, log tracks had to be built across it so that attackers with ladders could scale the walls.

Those who favored a safer approach climbed tall wooden towers, called belfries. These were wheeled up to the castle wall so that the soldiers inside could storm their way over.

GROUND LEVEL ATTACK

Attackers often tried to smash through a castle's gate or corner walls with a heavy metal-tipped tree trunk, called a battering ram. They also tried to batter down the castle's walls using mangonels and trebuchets.

The mangonel was powered by twisted ropes. It could hurl great weights, but not very accurately!

The trebuchet (a wooden catapult), on the other hand, was deadly accurate. Developed during the 1100s, it had a sling at one end and a heavy counterweight at the other. When the counterweight fell, the missile in the sling went hurtling toward its target.

A large trebuchet could throw a dead horse. Bombarding a castle with rotting remains helped to spread disease among the defenders. Being splattered by rotted horse flesh can't have done much for their morale either!

GOING UNDERGROUND

Castles without water-filled moats were vulnerable to tunneling. Enemy miners would tunnel under a wall, set fire to the wooden poles used to support the tunnel's roof, and then wait for both the tunnel and the wall above it to collapse.

A WAITING GAME

Attackers sometimes tried to starve their enemy into surrender by mounting a siege. They camped outside the castle and stopped food from being delivered.

Sieges were not always successful, though. A well-stocked castle could survive for months, and many attackers dared not leave their own castles undefended for that long.

23

FIRE YOUR OWN TREBUCHET

You will need: 2 blocks of balsa wood, 1 inch square and 8½ inches long ● a large sheet of balsa (¼ inch thick) ● a stick of balsa wood about 8½ inches long ● unsharpened round pencil ● small screw hook ● matchbox ● string ● pebble ● tape ● balsa cement ● craft knife ● small rubber band ● ruler ● paper.

Ask a grown-up to help you.

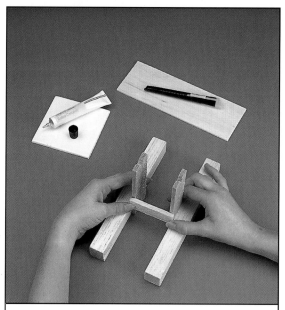

TO MAKE THE UPRIGHTS

1. Cut two pieces of balsa sheet, each measuring 4¼ inches by 1¼ inches. Carve a notch into one of the shorter sides of each piece. These notches must be wide enough and deep enough for the pencil to fit snugly into them.

▲**2.** Glue the uprights onto your two blocks of balsa wood, as shown. Make sure the notches line up with each other.

▲**3.** Cut a piece of balsa sheet 2¾ inches by ½ inch, and glue it across the front of the uprights. The position of this bar will affect your trebuchet's firing range.

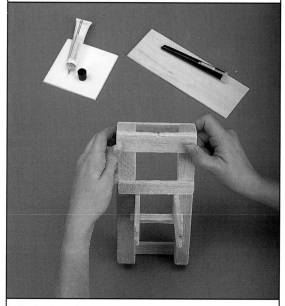

▲**4.** Cut four pieces of balsa sheet, each 4¼ inches by ¾ inch. Glue them, as shown, to complete the frame.

TO MAKE THE FIRING ARM

▲ **5.** Hold a pencil across your stick of balsa wood and fasten it with a rubber band. The pencil should be about a third of the way down the stick.

▲ **6.** Tape a pebble to the short end of the arm. Glue half a matchbox tray to the other end.

▲ **7.** Knot a length of string under the matchbox. Then tie a small loop in the string, near the knot.

▲ **8.** Screw a small hook into the back of the frame. Rest the arm on the uprights and pull it down so that you can slip the loop of string over the hook.

9. To fire your trebuchet, put a crumpled ball of paper into the matchbox and flick the string off the hook.

CASTLES IN DECLINE

European castles went out of fashion because the society that had needed them began to change. In England and Wales this happened during the 1400s. As the monarchy grew stronger, private wars between great lords became less frequent. Pitched battles fought in the open countryside became more common. Since the two sides were often fighting to control the whole country, capturing a castle and its lands was not so important.

When cannons became popular weapons, soldiers were paid to man specially built gun forts. Fortress homes with their tall towers and arrow slits were no longer needed.

The times were changing in other ways, too. The nobility now longed for more comfortable homes, with bigger windows to let in more light. Some started to alter their castles accordingly. Others built grand manor houses instead. These new homes often had moats, battlements and gatehouses, but they were more for show than defense.

Castles that weren't adapted to a new role were abandoned. They were either pulled down and their building materials used for something else, or they were just left to crumble away.

▲ *English gun fort, Deal, Kent, England.*

Coity Castle in Wales fell into disuse at the end of the 1500s. ▼

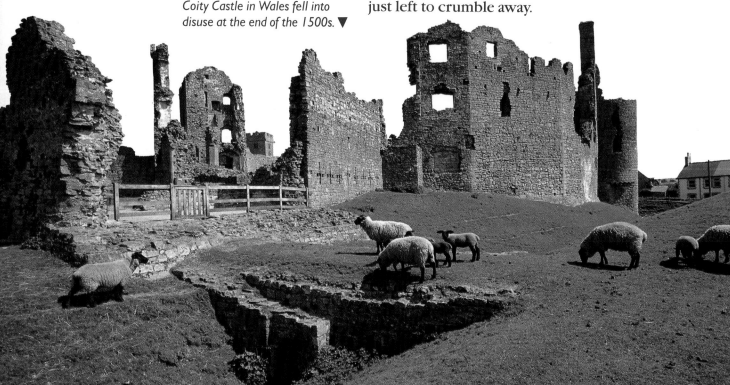

Castle building survived longer in Scotland, Ireland and other parts of Europe than in England and Wales. In fact, when cannons became effective siege weapons, some European castles were adapted to withstand their fire. Walls were thickened, towers were lowered and their flat roofs were used as cannon platforms.

However, as gunfire became more effective and central governments became more stable, castles in the rest of Europe fell out of favor, too. Rather than turn their homes into gloomy gun forts, the rich wanted to live in princely palaces and magnificent mansions.

▲ *François I of France began building this expensive palace at Chambord in 1519.*

During the 1700s and 1800s, fairytale-like castles became fashionable in parts of Europe. But, unlike the genuine castles of old, these were built for beauty, not defense.

▶ *Neuschwanstein Castle in Germany was built in 1869-92 by "Mad" King Ludwig II.*

CASTLES IN THE AIR

Castles have not only fascinated those interested in the past; they have spellbound storytellers, too. European myths and legends are full of tales about castles. The gods of Norse mythology lived in Asgard. This was a castle kingdom in the air, guarded by a massive rainbow bridge. The Welsh sea god, Manawyddan the Wise, lived in a castle made out of human bones.

Celtic mythology has many stories about castles buried beneath the sea. One myth recalls the watery fate of the castle of Ys, in Cornwall. The people of Ys grew so unbelievably wicked that one day the sea rose up and swallowed their castle and town. They would only be saved when a young man on the mainland heard the sad sound of the castle's chapel bell.

As castles disappeared from the real world, storytellers started inventing more and more weird and wonderful ones to take their place. Some are dark and disturbing, like the devilish castle created by the Italian writer, Dante. In his castle, everything is horribly reversed. The moat is a river of death. The burning hot walls are designed to keep people in, not out. The curtain walls spiral inward and downward to a pit filled with horrors.

Some of the most popular stories of all have real castles at their center. William Shakespeare's play *Macbeth* is set in Glamis Castle, in Scotland. His play *Hamlet* takes place at the royal castle of Elsinore, in Denmark.

Glamis Castle has a bloody history, both in fact and fiction. ▼

▲ Kronborg Castle in Denmark was made famous by the play Hamlet.

There is a German legend about a young man called Dietrich who rescues a princess from a dwarf king's castle, only to find that the ungrateful girl prefers her captor to him. The story goes that this castle can be found in the Tyrolean mountains. However, since only the pure and good can see it, it's unlikely that anyone has ever had a quick look inside!

29

GLOSSARY

Armorer — the man who took care of the castle's weapons and armor.

Barbican — some barbicans were like long walkways leading to the gatehouse. Others were like small gatehouses, built to protect the bridge leading to the main gatehouse.

Battering ram — a metal-tipped tree trunk or wooden pole, which was often suspended from the roof of a wooden shed on wheels. By swinging the ram back and forth against the castle's gate or corners, a team of men could smash their way through to the other side.

Battlements — a line of notches along the top of a tower or wall. Defending archers fired between the gaps, called crenels, and hid behind the higher bits of stonework, called merlons.

Belfries— tall wooden siege towers on wheels. They were often topped by a drawbridge and covered with animal hides for fireproofing.

Celts — an ancient race of people who came from western Britain, Wales, Ireland, Scotland and Brittany.

Château Gaillard — the favorite castle of King Richard I of England. It was built in the 1190s, on a cliff overlooking the River Seine, in France.

Curtain wall — general name given to the wall and towers surrounding a castle.

Legends — traditional stories that are part fact and part fiction. Myths and legends are handed down from one generation to the next.

Mangonel — a catapult used for throwing stones great distances when attacking a castle.

Myth — an ancient traditional story. Myths are often about gods and heroes. Many have a religious meaning, or try to explain some scientific fact.

Mythology — the study of myths; a collection of the myths and legends of a particular culture.

Norse mythology — the myths and legends of the Vikings, who came from Scandinavia.

Pitched battle — one that has been arranged and is fought on a chosen site.

Reed — a tall, stiff marsh or water grass.

Rushes — grasslike plants that grow near marshes.

Trebuchet — a large wooden catapult used when attacking a castle.

RESOURCES

BOOKS TO READ

Castles and Forts by Simon Adams (Boston; Kingfisher, 2003)

Castle by Peter Dennis (Hauppauge, NY; Barrons Juvenile, 2001)

Eyewitness: Castle by Christopher Gravett (New York; DK Publishing, 2000)

1-2-3 Draw Knights, Castles, and Dragons by Freddie Levin (London, Ontario; Peel Productions, 2001)

Castle by David Macaulay (Boston; Houghton Mifflin, 1982)

A Medieval Castle by Fiona Macdonald (Columbus, OH; Peter Bedrick Books, 1993)

Castles and Knights by Victoria Salley (New York; Prestel USA, 2001)

The Usborne Book of Castles by Lesley Sims (Tulsa, OK; Usborne Books, 2002)

Castles of the World Coloring Book by A. G. Smith (Mineola, NY; Dover, 1986)

Castles by Phillip Steele (Boston; Kingfisher, 1995)

ON THE WEB

www.castlesontheweb.com
  (Everything about castles)
www.castles-of-britain.com
  (Interactive guide to British castles)

Note to parents and teachers
Every effort has been made by the Publishers to ensure that the websites in this book are suitable for children, that they are of the highest educational value, and that they contain no inappropriate or offensive material. However, because of the nature of the Internet, it is impossible to guarantee that the contents of these sites will not be altered. We strongly advise that Internet access is supervised by a responsible adult.

The Metropolitan Museum of Art, The Cloisters
Fort Tryon Park
New York, NY 10040
(212) 923-3700

Among the displays to be seen here are medieval tapestries, metalwork, furniture, stained glass, and other artifacts from the Middle Ages.

West Point Museum, United States Military Academy
West Point, NY 10996
(914) 938-2203; (914) 938-3590

Several different types of arms, armor, and weapons are displayed.

INDEX

Additional photographs: Bridgeman Art Library/Private Collection 4(b); Danish Tourist Board 29(t); Michael Holford 26(t), 27(t); Hutchison Library 4(t); Science Museum 12(t); Wales Tourist Board 14, 26(b); Zefa 27(b), 29(b).